The Colored Lady Evangelist

John H. Acornley

WIPF & STOCK · Eugene, Oregon

Wipf and Stock Publishers
199 W 8th Ave, Suite 3
Eugene, OR 97401

The Colored Lady Evangelist
By Acornley, John H.
ISBN 13: 978-1-4982-9152-1
Publication date 2/25/2016
Previously published by Garland Publishing, Inc., 1892

THE COLORED LADY EVANGELIST,

—BEING THE—

Life, Labors and Experiences,

—OF—

MRS. HARRIET A. BAKER,

—BY—

Rev. John H. Acornley.

AUTHOR OF "SUNSHINE AMONG THE MOUNTAINS," &C.

"Go ye into all the world and preach the gospel to every creature."
Mark 16: 15.

CONTENTS.

PREFACE.

Mrs. Harriet A. Baker has had a very chequered experience. Starting life in what was little better than bondage she has struggled heroically against adverse circumstances, and by dint of indomitable perseverance has made herself a name, and won the respect of those who know her best. Having given herself to Christ in her youth, she early served the Saviour in a humble capacity, until called upon to enter into a wider sphere of usefulness, when she laid herself fully upon the altar of consecration, and went forth to proclaim the unsearchable riches of Christ. And now, after the lapse of more than a decade, which she has spent in evangelistic work, it has been deemed desirable to issue a brief account of her life, experience and work. At her request I have undertaken the work of preparation, and I pray that the Divine blessing may accompany it to the consciences and hearts of its readers, and that the ultimate result may be that the number of Zion's travelers may be augmented.

JOHN H. ACORNLEY.

60 PARK AVENUE,
Brooklyn, N. Y.

CHAPTER I.

BIRTH, PARENTAGE AND EARLY LIFE.

Christian biography has often been blessed of God in the reclaimation amd salvation of those who have been living at variance with his will, and in violation of his law. Blasphemers and persecutors have been led, by the quiet perusal of the record of the inner lives of God's children, to change their sentiments and conduct, to open their hearts to the influence of the Divine Spirit, and to realize and experience that change which we call conversion. God's word declares that "the righteous shall be in everlasting rememberance," thus we perceive that the effort to preserve from oblivion the characters and experiences of good men and women is in harmony with the will of God. Examples of holy living and devoted service are far more potent for good than the most powerful preaching, not that we would say anything, that would lessen the institution of preaching in the estimation of the readers of these pages; but the minds and hearts of the mass of men and women are moved far more readily by what persons are, than by what they say. We trust that this humble record of the labors and experiences of Mrs. Baker may result in good to countless numbers who are now walking in the "broad way" to ruin.

Harriet Ann Baker, whose maiden name was Cole, was born in Havre de Grace, Harford County, Maryland. A town of about 2,500 inhabitants, situated on the right bank of the Susquehanna River, and at the entrance into the Chesapeake Bay. The time of her advent into this world was about the year 1829.

She was the daughter of William and Harriet Cole. Her great-grandmother, on the maternal side was an Indian squaw, who was married to an Englishman. They had a daughter who married a man of the name of Lego, a native of Guinea, who resided on the Bush River Neck, and whose daughter Harriet was Mrs. Baker's mother.

Her grandmother on the paternal side (whose maiden name was Bradford) was a slave, and was employed as cook in a slaveholder's family. She had meanwhile married a man of the name of Cole. (Still she was best known by her maiden name Bradford.) She was a highspirited woman, and would not quietly submit under any circumstances to be whipped. She was gentle, tractable, reliable, and industrious, when allowed to perform her duties in peace, and not subjected to the indignity of the whipping post.

For some cause she was sold, and her new

mistress, being one of those haughty imperious dames, who regarded her slaves as but so much chattel property, for some trivial cause had her whipped. This roused the tiger spirit of rebellion within her, and shortly after she took the cow-hide and applied it vigorously across the shoulders of her mistress, who had done something to offend her. When her master came home, and found his wife in bed, he was so enraged that, after knocking Mrs. Bradford down, he sent for the overseer and had her tied to the post, and the long whip was applied with such dreadful power, that strips of skin and flesh were brought away from her quivering body, with every stroke of the lash. Blood flowed freely, but still gash after gash was cut, until by the time they had finished their dreadful work, her very entrails had protruded.

A gentleman passing at the time was attracted by hearing the cries and shrieks of the wretched victim, and immediately ran in, and cut her down. Her body fell across the axe which was lying on the floor. but with a super-human energy, she sprang to her feet, and with the ferocity and strength of a demon, seized the axe, and split the skull of her brutal master, killing him instantly. Then she turned furiously upon the overseer, and struck him a blow from which he died in a couple of days.

She was taken to Baltimore to jail. The case was of such a revolting nature that the citizens took it in hand, and interested themselves in her behalf. She was carried into court on a couch, and the result of the trial was, she was acquitted and granted her freedom. About five weeks after her arrest, while lying in jail awaiting her trial, she gave birth to her son William.

After her liberation she was in very poor circumstances, and found the struggle exceedingly hard to support herself and child. When the boy became old enough to be of some use, she bound him out to a slave owner, until he should be twenty-five years of age. He grew up to be a tall, powerful, square-built young fellow; he stood over six feet high and was proportionately stout and strong. He was known as Bill Bradford, (his mother's maiden name.)

He became noted as a prize fighter, and in this was encouraged by his master, who having staked, and won a considerable amount of money on his numerous pugilistic encounters, manifested his appreciation by setting William free when nineteen years of age. From this time until his marriage with Miss Harriet Lego, he resided with his mother in Baltimore, and provided for her wants.

Mrs. Baker's educational privileges were very small, indeed she never went to school one hour in her life. At that time there were no colored schools. Indeed it was considered a high offense to teach a colored child to read. We will give her own account, she says:

"No mortal man or woman on earth has taught me a letter, I grew up without it. After I was married, I studied to learn the letters. I cannot forget how, at one time, when I was living at a rich gentleman's house, and I was obliged to clean out his office. I saw a letter on his table, and wanting to write very much, I took up the pen, and copied from his letter, and put the duplicate in my pocket, but I could not read it, so I carried it around in my pocket until it was worn out. I did not know A from B, but I could copy all I saw, and I was very quick to learn."

What a change has been wrought in a few years! Now schools are built and maintained, and duly qualified teachers appointed and supported for the special purpose of teaching the colored child, not only the rudiments, but all the branches of an advanced education.

Although free born, she had many hardships to meet with in her early life. Her father died when she was only eleven years and four months old. In regard to this period in her life, she says:

"It was the custom for the slaveholder to come in as soon as the man was dead, not to give the widow money or bread, but to lay hold on the children which were old enough to work, and bind them out. I do thank God that my mother stood up for her children. My mother was left with seven. Three out of that number were wanted, but it was the law that if they had plenty of provisions and clothes in the house they could not take the children. They searched the house about a dozen times, but did not find it empty. I thank God that the meal, flour, potatoes, meat and fish barrels were full, as by that means, I with the rest of the children, were saved. They did not want the little ones, as they could not work, so some of the friends that my father worked for, (though they were slaveholders) pitied us, and sent us five bushels of corn, three bushels of wheat, and some meat every winter; besides which the largest of us would at times go out to service, so by that means I was saved from slavery.

The agents of slaveholders were constantly on the watch, and if they could quietly kidnap a young colored person, they would hurry them away, and sell them into slavery, and if intercepted, and remonstrated with, they would charge the unfortunate with having run away from bondage, or with having stolen something.

In order to secure her child from the cruel kidnappers, Mrs. Baker's mother, hired her out at first for one dollar per month, and when ever she changed places, her mother would bring her away and strip her in the presence of the lady, shaking open all her clothes, so that they might not be able to say that she had stolen anything, or taken anything in her clothes. Says Mrs. Baker:

"God blessed me with a good wise mother, and I feel more than thankful to the Lord that mother hired me out at one dollar and twenty-five cents per month, to Mrs. Bailey, where I stayed a long while. I had it very pleasant there, for as the madam nad no children they took quite a fancy to me, as much as though I was a child of their own. The lady visitors used to tell the madam that they did not see why she made such a fuss over a little colored child. She would then get angry, and I would get angry too. She would take her silk dresses and tuck them up for me, and I tell you, I used to feel big."

CHAPTER II.

MARRIAGE AND SETTLEMENT ON FREE SOIL.

"Marriage is honorable in all," so says the great Apostle of the Gentiles, and therefore the institution is not to be lightly esteemed. There have, however, been some modern teachers who have attempted to prove that this Divine institution is a failure, and they have held up as illustrations to substantiate their position, cases, where the parties have been unable to live in harmony with each other, where domestic quarrels have been engendered, and separations and divorces the final result. But then, they seem to forget, or ignore the fact altogether, that history proves that those nations who have held the marriage bond in light esteem have gradually loosened their grip upon those influences which hold people together in civilized communities. And that in order to be virtuous it is essential to have a proper conception of the solemnity and importance of all nuptial ties.

Marriage should not be a civil contract merely, but it should be the result of genuine affection, then it may be expected that the Divine blessing will rest upon the union, and domestic happiness will surely follow.

Mrs. Baker was married October 25th, 1845, when only seventeen years of age, to William Baker, a slave. She was ambitious to excell in all her duties, and would not let anyone outstrip her in working, and hence her services were in much demand. At one large house where she was employed there were fourteen in the family, she had fourteen cows to milk, and the dairy to attend to, besides her house work. This was the reason that Mr. Edward Gallop (Baker's owner) so readily consented to their marriage.

He conceived the idea that by this means her interest would be identical with that of his house, that he would be able to secure her services for a very nominal sum, if not without wages altogether, and that she would be ready at his beck and call. He encouraged the young people, and endeavoured to excite their vanity by arranging for a notice of their marriage to appear in the local paper. And says Mrs. Baker:

"It did make me feel quite big to see my name in the paper, and especially as two of the first families in the town were to be married, and the notice of their marriage would appear at the same time."

The second year after their marriage, in 1847, Mrs. Baker learned that for some cause or other, her husband's owner had detemined to sell him to a Georgian trader. Such occurrances were frequent, and they would endeavor to pacify the friends of the victim by inventing some story about their having run away, or being drowned. She heard of the plans through a friend of the master's wife, and of course she was wrought up to a very high pitch of excitement, and determined if possible to circumvent this design.

Her husband could scareely believe that his master had any intention of selling him, and he wanted to make some inquiry, but she would not allow it, for that would only have precipitated the crisis, and made escape impossible. However, though less vigorous and energetic than his amiable spouse, he was nevertheless anxiously desirous to escape out of the hands of the cruel slave trader.

It had been arranged by his master to send him away on Monday morning, but on Saturday evening, about midnight they struck out for liberty. She with her first born in her arms, a little over seven weeks old. They walked all that night and the next day (Sunday), they toiled on for forty-eight miles, until they finally crossed the border into the State of Pennsylvania, and at last breathed the air of perfect freedom.

According to that immortal document, the Declaration of Independance, of which every true American is proud, every person has been endowed by the Great Creator "with certain inalienable rights," and those rights are life! liberty! and happiness! no one has any right to deprive another of the opportunity, or the means, by which they shall live. Everyone has the right to eat the bread which their own hands earn, without asking anybody else's leave. Liberty is the birthright of every human being, and everyone ought to have the opportunity of seeking happiness in any legitimate way without let or hindrance.

But in those days this grand principle was not universally recognized, human slavery was regarded as a Divine institution; nor was it until about twenty-five years ago, when our rulers "cried havoc, and let slip the dogs of war," that the rights of colored people were in some measure recognized, and they were allowed that freedom which had so long been denied them.

Two sections of this great nation struggled and tore at each others throats, trampled down fields, destroyed towns, and slew each other, thus illustrating the truth that

"Man's inhumanity to man
Makes countless thousands mourn."

But the result was that four million slaves went forth to freedom, and Miriam's song, on the occasion of the Egyptian discomfiture, was sung by an enraptured and emancipated people through every section of the Southern States.

"Sound the loud timbrel, o'er Egypt's dark sea,
Jehovah has triumphed, His people are free."

They settled in Columbia, Lancaster County, Pennsylvania, strangers among strange people, with a capital of less than ten cents to begin life afresh, and sustain themselves and their helpless babe.

Columbia is located in an important lumber region, and had at that time a population of about 8,000 souls.

Mrs. Baker and her husband went to work with a will. In those days work was plentiful, and men could get a good price for their labor. Says Mrs. Baker:

"I shall never forget the first money that my husband earned. He got five dollars, and I said to him, 'not five dollars old man? ugh! my gracious now, ugh! we can get all that we want with that! ugh!' but when we started out to buy groceries, dry-goods, furniture etc., to our surprise, the man wanted six dollars for half a dozen chairs. O my! It was enough to make me faint! We wanted to buy everything at once, but was unable to purchase more than the dry-goods and groceries. The next money that he earned was ten dollars and we went to a sale and bought some furniture, and still I had five dollars in change left, with which to lay in our weeks stock of groceries. You would have laughed if you could have seen him bring in the next ten dollars. I could not see what use I could make of it, so I told Baker that we ought to buy property with it, as we were getting old, and wanted something to live on in our old days. He agreed to everything I said. Things are very different now, he does not mind me so much as he used to, for he has got very hard-headed since then."

Their object was to secure for themselves a home, and this they accomplished after a great deal of labor and self-denial.

They secured a lot of ground from Dr. Clarkson, who kindly gave them possession on the payment of $5.00 as a deposit. They then contracted with Mr. Sutton, Mr. Wrighter and Mr. Goans, for lumber, stone and lime—these gentlemen furnishing the material on very easy terms.

The good Lord raised up friends for them on every hand, so that in the Spring of 1848, the frame of the house having been reared, the doors and windows hung, and the roof put on, they moved into it, and then lathed, plastered, painted and papered it themselves.

The God whom they trusted still blessed them, and though they had to work almost night and day, yet He gave them strength to accomplish their purpose, so that at the end of three years they had all the debt paid off their new home, except a small amount on the ground.

In the Fall of 1850 the fugitive slave bill passed, giving the slaveholder the right to pursue his slaves into the Northern States, and take his property back into bondage.

> "Nor yet, O Freedom! close thy lids
> In slumber; for thine enemy never sleeps."
>
> —*Bryant.*

In the excitement which prevailed in consequence of the passage of this bill, hundreds of colored people left their homes, and sought more permanent safety in Canada. Among the rest Mr. Baker started off, but did not get any further than Boston; from thence he returned as far as New York, and finding his brother, stayed with him, and commenced work on Front street with a firm of wholesale grocers, of the name of "Swift and Waldon." He then sent for his wife, and she joined him in November. Here they stayed eight weeks, when, on the advice of some friends in Columbia they returned home. Those friends promising that in case of his being seized they would stand by her, and if money would buy him back they would assist her. They reasoned that if he was captured in New York, as scores of others were, he might be taken down South before assistance could reach him. They arrived home in the latter part of December. Mrs. Baker was troubled continually in her waking and sleeping hours, she was filled with a constant dread, and kept him in the house. She would not even let him go out to get a drink of water.

About three weeks after their return home the town was full of strange and suspicious looking men. She was convinced they were agents of the slaveholders, who were prowling around ready to pounce upon any unwary one, and drag them off.

One day, having promised to saw a quarter of a cord of wood for a gentleman, Mr. Baker got his saw and was about to leave the house, when his wife tried by persuasion and by physical force to detain him; she struggled and wrestled with him, and assured him that if he went out, he would certainly be taken, as she had been greatly troubled in her sleep, had dreamt about his capture, and had actually seen him fall into their hands. But he did not heed her and finally broke loose, and ran down the stairs with saw in hand, laughingly calling out that he would be back in a little while. He had not been gone more than twenty minutes before he was caught.

The local constable accompanied by three or four strange men, arrested him on the charge of being concerned in a riot at Lancaster.

He protested that he had not been to Lancaster.

The constable said, "I know you are not the man, they have the wrong name on the warrant, but just go down to the squire's office, and report, and it will be all right, you can then go back to your work."

Mr. Baker suspected nothing until they came near the office, when some one called him to stop, and looking around he saw the streets full of people.

His captors rushed upon bim and handcuffed him, and then he realized that he was in the hands of the slaveholders minions.

When Mrs. Baker got the news she rushed out and told her brother, who ran along with her until they reached Second Street. At the corner of Second and Locust Streets they separated, he went down Locust and she down Walnut Street.

When he got to Front and Locust he met a host of men, he fought his way through, but before he got the distance of half a block he was knocked down, kicked in the neck, and wounded in the head, from the effects of which he never fully recovered; his brain was affected, and, he was never entirely himself again.

When she got to the corner of Walnut and Third, she found the street blockaded with people, hundreds of rough fellows had come from the surrounding towns at the call, and in the pay, of the slaveholders agents, to assist them should there be any attempt on the part of the citizens to rescue their victims out of their hands. People screamed, and the excitement on every hand was intense.

With the combined help of some of her friends, she elbowed her way through the crowd, and finally got to the Squire's office. The crowd tried to hold her back, but like a wild tigress, she jumped at the door, burst it open, and with a terrific wild whoop she swept into the office. She was knocked down, and flung unconsicious on a pile of wood. When she came to, she raged and fumed, and tore around like a wild creature, which indeed she was. In the confusion some one threw a brick, which struck the constable, and thinking it was Mrs. Baker a number of them rushed at her with their loaded revolvers; they snapped them, but they would not go off. Thus did Divine providence mercifully interpose in her behalf in preventing them imbruing their hands in her blood.

Some readers may be ready to doubt the veracity of this statement and may say that in her frenzy her imagination would conjure up the most unlikely circumstances: and that even supposing the pistols did snap and refuse to go off, it was purely accidental and not a divine interposition in her behalf. But Mrs. Baker solemnly affirms that such was the fact, she distinctly saw them load and reload and take aim, and heard the snap of the trigger, and she firmly believes that He who holds all things in the hollow of His hands interposed to deliver her. And why should it be thought a thing incredable that God should interpose in behalf of his people? He who delivered the three Hebrew worthies from the burning fiery furnace, and who saved his servant Daniel from the rapacious jaws of the lions, often interferes in behalf of his own.

All this time a train stood in waiting, her husband was thrown aboard and they steamed off immediately. Meanwhile she had been knocked down two or three times by some unknown persons, but she sprang to her feet and ran frantically after in the vain endeavor to overtake it, and if it were possible upset the whole train, and throw cars and locomotive altogether into the Susquehanna river. And at that moment she felt strong enough for the undertaking. Some kind friend took charge of her, and led her home, but the state of her mind can be imagined better than expressed. And yet she felt confident that God would help her.

Mr. Baker was taken to Philadelphia for trial, the trial lasted four days, Lawyer Paul Brown pleaded his case, but he was condemned as a fugitive slave, and given back to his master.

$750.00 in gold was demanded as the price of his redemption. Gold at that time was worth about $1.90, his master had been offered $1400.00 for him down south, which was about equivalent to $750.00 in gold.

Mr. Shuck, cashier at the bank kindly came to her aid at the request of four citizens who took the matter in hand and advanced the required sum, taking as security a mortgage on the home they had laboured so hard to get together. The money was sent on Saturday, and Mr. Baker was brought back on a special train on Sunday. The town was very much excited. After she found that it was really her husband returned to her safe a terrible reaction came over her, she took sick, and for several weeks lay between life and death. While in this condition she was confined, but her infant died in nine days.

O how gracious and good is our benificent Father, says he, "I will never leave thee, nor forsake thee" "Lo I am with you alway."

In mercy she was restored to health and many times since has she had cause to thank and bless God for his mercy and grace.

The following is the testimony of S. Evans Esq., Justice of the Peace, as to the credibility of the story of events just related.

"I, Samuel Evans, Justice of the Peace, in and for Columbia, Lancaster County, Pa., do hereby certify from personal knowledge that William Baker, (colored, husband of Rev. Harriet A. Baker, Evangelist,) was arrested under the fugitive slave law in this town in 1851 and remanded back into slavery.

"Several hundred dollars were raised by a number of citizens to purchase his freedom. When he returned to this town he mortgaged his little home to raise money to reimburse those who purchased his freedom. His house burned down, and after many years of hard struggling he paid off that debt of honor, which left him poor, and with an encumbrance of several hundred dollars of debt on his homestead.

"For several years he has been totally disabled from work on account of chronic rheumatism. He was the first slave who was captured and sent back to slavery under the law of 1850. He is a sober and worthy colored man, and any charity bestowed on him will not go to an unworthy person.

Columbia, Pa.

Nov. 12, 1888.

SAMUEL EVANS.

J. P."

On account of sickness. and death in the family, it took six years hard toil to redeem their property again, but they worked with a will, and at the end of that period were rewarded with success.

In February 1863 some evil disposed person or persons set fire to their house, and it was burnt to the ground. All that they had was destroyed, and they were compelled to begin again, where they had started sixteen years before. They were certainly greatly discouraged, but with the assistance of kind friends who again came to their help, they soon rebuilt, and were getting along very nicely, paying off their indebtedness, when death entered their home, and took away one of their dear children. This was a heavy stroke, but was succeded by another, which almost prostrated them. That was the death, within two weeksof each other of two very interesting girls aged thirteen and fifteen years respectively. They both left a clear testimony behind that they were going to be with Jesus.

Hannah Rebecca the eldest, just before she died said, "I am ready and willing to go," and then calling her mother to her bed-side she said, "Mother death can't harm me as long as Jesus is near me, and Jesus is near me now." When asked if she was afraid of the grave, or if she regretted leaving her friends, her answer was, "No, you must follow me." And with a promise from mother to meet her at the throne she took her flight and winged her way to heaven, March 20th, 1872.

Rulletta Stephen died on the 9th of April, a little over two weeks after her sister. One of her little school-mates came to see her, and she counseled her to pray, and be good, for said she "Jesus says, suffer little children to come unto me and forbid them not for of such is the kingdom of heaven," and stretching out her hands, she said "O, if I had wings I would fly." Then she spoke of the meeting with her sister in the happy land, and urged her mother to hurry and follow after. And the result of the dying testimony of this dear child was that one hundred souls were converted.

These are ties which are continually drawing the mother to the land of light. And by and by we trust, when her life work here is ended, she will go sweeping through the pearly gates, and greet her children amid the dazzling glories of the new Jerusalem.

"O when thou city of my God
Shall I thy courts ascend,
Where congregations ne'er break up,
And Sabbaths have no end."

CHAPTER III.

CONVERSION.

Mrs. Baker was converted in the year 1842, when about twelve or thirteen years of age. We will give the account in her own words. "Mr. Bailey, with whom I was in service for a long while, was a dancing master, and got up all the large balls for the children of the rich; he trained me to dance, and oh! how delighted I was when the time came to go to the balls. I was always the first on the floor.

One day my mother asked me if I wanted to go to a band-meeting, and I replied, "yes, ma'm. She then told me to come home on a certain night and she would take me along. My sister and another girl went with us. I put on my best dress, rings, curls and jewelry to go to the band-meeting. I thought it must be something grand, or mother would not ask me to go with her. I knew we had bands and music at the balls, so I was delighted at the prospect. When we had gone to the outside of the town I asked mother how much further we had to go, but she only told me to come along, and that was enough for me, I knew better than to say anything, so we traveled on about five miles, when we came to a farm which nobody lived upon, except a colored family, who were there to watch the place. There was a dirt floor, a few old stools and benches, and a long pine table, upon which was a tin plate, containing lard for oil, and rags for wick, and which was burning in place of a lamp. I sat down, but I did not know what to do, my clothes were my study, and I waited for the band. I could not see, however, how they were going to get along in such a place. After awhile the women began to come in, two or three at a time, until there was about sixteen of them. Then they got up and locked the door, and put a great bar across. I could not tell what it meant, so I watched them until they commenced the meeting. Then you may depend I was cross with myself to think that I had only come to a prayer-meeting. The meeting progressed, and I was so afraid of getting my clothes dirty that I didn't know what to do. They sang and prayed until it began to get awful warm in the room, and then down fell the two girls in the dirt. I couldn't understand it at all. I looked with all my might and thought that they must all be crazy. After awhile they all got down on their knees, and prayed, and sang, and when they rose, I was so sick that I could hardly stand up. I shook all over and said to myself, the reason those girls fell down was because they were sick with the heat.' It was so warm, that I thought if I didn't get some cool air, I should fall down too. I reached out my hand to my mother, and pulled her dress to attract her attention, and asked her to please open the door, and let me out; but she just turned her back upon me, and went right on singing. What to do I did not know, but I made up my mind that I wouldn't get down upon my knees again, for if I did, I thought, I should never be able to get up.

I was also afraid of getting my clothes soiled in the dirt, I got close to the jam, that is the fire-place, and leaned against it, and looking up I saw a brick out of place, and reaching up my two hands I passed them in there, determined to hold on until the praying was over, and then perhaps I might be able to get outside. But I tell you the power of God struck me down. I thought that I was in a dark and black pit, and when I came to myself I was so far down, that I knew no mortal hand could reach me. I cried out with all my heart to Jesus, the way I heard my mother do, but I did not know who he was, or where he was. I believed, however, he could catch me before I got to that awful place. I did not believe that anyone else could get to me, so I called to him with all my might, and he heard me. Oh, what a bright light he brought to me! It was a glorious light, which was accompanied with the sweetest of peace. I cannot forget what trouble and sorrow I was in, for I could not find anything to catch hold of, and help myself out. I was reaching aud grasping all about to find something to hold on to, but in vain. I called on Jesus so earnestly that, glory to God! he took right hold of me, and saved me by his grace. Ah! I tell you he came in power! Now I want to tell you that if I hadknown anything about God or his Word it would have been quite different, but I did not. I had only heard mother, and some other old women talking, and praying to Jesus. But that night, praise God! He saved my soul, and I praise God continually for his goodness and mercy to me from that time to the present. He taught me by his spirit to read his holy Word, and not only to read it, but to understand it also. I can say with all my soul that I praise God for what he has done for me. It is now about forty-eight years since Jesus found me, a poor little girl, blind in sin, and dancing my way down to hell, not knowing anything about God or the Bible; but he saved me in time, and brought me into his fellowship, and made me one of his family. Glory to his dear name!"

That little log cabin, on the old Bay farm, where those few women met to pray will never be forgotten. The remembrance of that evening's devotions will live in Mrs. Baker's memory as long as life shall last. There she was made a new creature in Christ Jesus, and started on that heavenly journey which will terminate only at the throne.

CHAPTER IV.

CALL TO EVANGELISTIC WORK.

Mrs. Baker was long impressed with the conviction that it was the Lord's will that she should enter upon some distinctive work for him. She observed thousands perishing around her, and she felt she must go out and speak to the people, tell them of the love of Jesus, and warn them to flee from the wrath to come. For some time she hesitated, afraid to venture. The work appeared so fearfully momentous, and she realizing her own weakness, cast herself before the Lord in humble supplication and prayer. She wrestled with God, but the more earnestly she prayed, and the clearer her conviction became that it was her duty to go, believing she would be sustained by Divine power.

It has already been stated that Mrs. Baker was unable to read or write until the Lord graciously spoke peace to her soul, and then inspired by the spirit she thirsted for information, and sought to be able to read the Book Divine, that in the quiet of her own room she might drink in its contents, and become imbued with its spirit, and thereby fitted for her great life work. She realized her own weakness, and called earnestly and loudly upon God for direction and deliverance. God opened her way. and in a wonderful manner directed her steps.

On one occasion she dreamed she was in the middle of a great sea, out of sight of land, standing on a platform, with nothing to be seen but the blue sky above and the deep waters beneath, the sea gently swelled until the platform upon which she stood floated away to a place just large enough to rest her two feet upon. As she stood there she called upon God for help, and as she prayed the Battery (a small vessel used by the fishermen in the Chesapeake Bay and on which, in company with another sister she had come to this place) floated away. and she was left alone looking up to the heavens for help. and as she looked. she saw a small cord coming down out of the clouds, and swinging lower and lower until it got within her reach; She imagined she heard a voice say "lay hold," but she was afraid. and hesitated. As she hesitated the cord swung to the south. and as it passed her, she thought she heard the voice say again "lay hold" and thus it continued to swing from north to south. She cried mightily for help. and again she heard the voice say "lay hold," her fears vanished in a moment, and as the cord passed her again, with a mighty effort she sprang and laid hold with both her hands. Conciousness left her, and she was carried away to the north, and when she came to herself, found that she had been set down in a strange land, among strange people, and she imagined she heard the same voice command her to tell the multitude of her wonderful deliverance and with a heart overflowing with gratitude and joy, she recounted in the hearing of the people who she had been so graciously delivered from the sea.

To a cold calculating philosophical reader these revelations may appear incredulous, but let it be remembered that however they may appear to others, to Mrs. Baker they were intensely real.

She met with considerable opposition, the members of the church to which she belonged intimated that God never intended women to preach the gospel: her pastor declaimed against her in the pulpit, and expostulated with her in private; her friends all tried to disuade her from her purpose; and her husband did all he could to prevent her; said he on one occasion, pointing to their two promising girls:

"If you leave these girls, and anything happens to them, it would be a stain on your character as long as you live, and I'll never forgive you."

For a time Mrs. Baker yielded to the great pressure which was brought to bear upon her, she staid home, and made the subject a matter of prayer. In her distress she told the Lord she could not go on account of these girls. And now it seemed as though a very whirlwind of trouble overtook her.

The two girls, Hannah Rebecca and Rulletta Stephen, the pride of their parents hearts, were seized by the ruthless hand of affliction, and after a short but painful struggle the death angel came and removed them away (within two weeks of each other) to the "land beyond," where they are undoubtedly "watching and waiting the appearance of their beloved parents at the "beautiful gate," and where beneath the tree of life, on the banks of the river of Paradise, they will joyfully recount to each other the way the good Lord has been so graciously leading them, and realizing that he has done all things well, they will cast their given crowns at their Redeemer's feet, and with pealing anthems of adoration, and swelling choruses of praise, they will unite with the blood-washed throng in crowning him Lord of all.

Mrs. Baker saw, or believed she saw, in this dispensation of Divine providence, the hand of God pointing the way. She fell to the ground as one dead, and when she regained consciousness she heard a voice which seemed to say, "Go now or you shall die.'' She bowed in humble submission and gave up all to the Lord. Three times she was herself afflicted so severely that her friends thought surely she would die, her sickness was of a complicated character, heart, kidney and liver complaints, with dyspepsia in its worst stages. Every effort was made for her recovery, all the physicians in the neighborhood were called in, but their skill was exercised in vain, she called earnestly upon God and promised faithfully if he would graciously restore her to health she would follow wheresoever he would lead. The Lord mercifully heard her prayer and completely restored her, and in her heart she gave praise for His goodness.

The opposition to her entering upon evangelistic work was still not subdued, preacher and people, husband and children, her best and dearest friends, acted as though they were combined to stop her from going, but she was so sure of her Divine commission that she held fast to her purpose.

One evening, at the class-meeting, she made an appeal in her own behalf, and told how the Lord had so wonderfully led her. When she sat down her class-leader rose to his feet and gave utterance to a terrible tirade of abuse. She was cut to the quick, the tempter suggested that she should leave the church, and never set foot in it again. Still she remembered David's declaration that "the steps of the good man (or woman) are ordered by the Lord, and he delighted in his way." She thought she heard a voice encouraging her to stand still and see the salvation of God. The voice appeared to say, "Didn't you promise the Lord you would never run away, though the struggle might be fierce and hot? Do not falter' be of good courage, I will fight your battles." With uplifted hands and heart, she had truly made this promise to the Lord in secret. Her friends knew nothing of this solemn covenant, but God sustained her. While the war of words was going on in the church, she kept her seat, and with bowed head, held secret communion with God. She said, "Oh! Lord, if thou intends to deliver me, if thou intends that I should be successful in my work, let it please thee to make it known again here to-night. I know that Thou hast called and chosen me to this work, but these people don't know it. Lord let the people know it here and now." And the Lord did manifest himself in such power that the opposition was disarmed. Although they did not authorize her to preach until two years afterwards, yet their opposition ceased. As she sat in the church in great distress of mind she imagined herself carried away in the spirit to the summit of calvary, where she saw three crosses, on the centre one was suspended the world's Redeemer. the two thieves hung one on either side of Him. It was night. midnight darkness prevailed all around, which was only relieved by a stream of light over the Saviour's head. Here and there a straggler might be observed lingering near the cross. and a horseman armed with a spear (probably one of the Roman guard) stood near by. She imagined she stood in a field, and as she stood, she observed the road winding around the mountain. At a little distance there was a grove or piece of woods, and she saw herself wending her way, accompanied by a guide, towards those woods. She was told that her guide was no other than Simon, the Cyrenian, who had borne the Saviour's cross, and who was now making his way back to the hill country from whence he came.

And as they walked, suddenly a bright light shone from the east. She gazed at it with wonder, and saw rise before her an exceedingly high mountain, such as she had never seen before, she imagined its peaks reached to the very clouds. Behind this mountain was a great reflection which lit up both the heavens and the earth. And as she stood gazing in astonishment at the marvelous light, she imagined she saw the Lord Jesus standing on the top of the mountain clothed in bright raiment, with a glorious crown upon his head, streams of light flowing therefrom in dazzling rays. It was such a glorious sight as she had never seen before, and never expects to see again until she basks in the sunlight of her Redeemer's presence, amid the regal splendors of the New Jerusalem.

The Saviour looked upon her with a smile she will never forget, and spoke to her in a voice mellowed with sweetness. He reminded her of how He had delivered Joshua, and assured her He was the Captain of the host which had come to deliver her. She realized that He was the same God to-day, was filled with Divine glory, and springing to her feet she gave full expression to the joy of her soul. She praised

God who had revealed such wonderful things to her, and shouted glory! glory! glory!

The house was filled with the Divine presence, friends and foes felt and realized the power of God.

Her sister (who had been one of the most violent opposers) came to her in haste, and asked her if she did not see the lightening streaming through the church.

Her husband who was at home in bed felt the shock, as did others throughout the town. So the universal cry the next day was "loose the woman, and let her go."

Thus the Lord brought her out with a strong hand and a mighty arm, and in a short time afterwards she was enabled to enter upon her mission.

CHAPTER V.

ABUNDANT LABORS.

Having consecrated herself entirely to the Lord, time, talents, body and soul, Mrs. Baker commenced to make preparations for entering upon her great work.

One morning, in the Winter of 1872, she went up stairs, in the absence of her husband, and gathered a few collars and handkerchiefs together, made them into a small bundle, and leaving her three children (aged respectively four, six, and eight years) at home, she started (as Abraham did when he left his native land) not knowing where she went, but determined to follow in the way the Spirit directed, and leave everything else in the hands of God. She took the train and went as far as Acton Station, a little country place, where the depot stood in a lonely situation, no houses being near.

After the train had departed the gentlemanly station agent enquired where she was going.

Mrs. Baker replied that she was "looking for a preacher."

He told her there was no church within six or seven miles, and as the snow was very deep he was afraid she would freeze before she got there. He went out, but in a few minutes returned with another gentleman, who he had providentally seen going to the next town—a German settlement called Brownstown.

Mr. Getts, the last named gentleman, was a butcher, and having sold his meat was on his way home. He had a large sleigh, and kindly agreed to take Mrs. Baker along with him. When they arrived at Brownstown, seeing that she was not acquainted with either preacher or people, he generously took her to his home, and after supper went over with her to the church and introduced her to the pastor, Rev. Mr. Brown, of the Evangelical Church.

Mrs. Baker firmly believes that she was directed by the Holy Spirit to enter upon her mission IN THIS MANNER AND IN THIS PLACE, and wonderfully did the Lord show her the way. The people's hearts were opened to receive her. The minister invited her to stay at his house, and the people seemed to vie with each other in their hearty invitations to come and stay with them. She arranged to stay a day and night with each of them. They commenced a protracted meeting forthwith, which was continued for three weeks, the result being that SEVENTY-TWO SOULS were savingly converted and added to the church At the close of her three weeks labors she returned home leaving SEVEN MORE SOULS convicted of sin, and, at the altar of God, seeking remission therefrom.

Such was Mrs. Baker's first introduction into active evangelistic word. She had gone out without any human authority, the church, as has already been stated, being opposed to female evangelists did not grant her a license to preach until two years afterwards. Seeing, however, that she was being received in the white churches, and, better still, that the Divine approbation was so clearly manifest, that sinners were being converted, that believers were being edified, and that churches were being revived, the prejudice gradually subsided, and the way was made clear for her to labor among the churches of her own people.

In the Summer of 1874 a colored camp-meeting was held in a large grove in the vicinity of Cressona, a thriving little town of about 1500 inhabitants, in Schuylkill County, Pennsylvania.

This town was first called West Haven, but was subsequently changed to Cressona, in honor of John C. Cresson, the owner of the land upon which the town was built, and who was also the President of the Mine Hill and Schuylkill Haven Rail-Road.

To this camp-meeting special trains were run, and thousands of people came for miles around. It was estimated that on a Sabbath about sixteen thousand people were on the grounds. At the morning collection $130.00 was raised towards the minister's salary, the Holy Spirit was poured out in a copious manner, and great numbers of souls were graciously and lovingly saved from all sin.

As she stood before the people on this camp-ground, enjoying the beautiful scenery by which they were surrounded, she was forcibly reminded of the remarkable dream she had twenty-six years before, and which we recorded in the last chapter. How she was taken up from the sea by a cord; and how she was put down in the north, in a strange part of the country, in the midst of a multitude of people, and in the wilderness; and how she was told to stand up and tell of her deliverance from the sea. And as she stood before that vast concourse of people, it suddenly flashed across her mind that truly this was the place she had seen during the night watches, so many years before. And she greatly rejoiced that such large numbers were here, both white and colored, seeking the Saviour and realizing salvation.

It was while at this camp-meeting that she received an invitation to labor in the St. Clair, Pottsville and Mahanoy City Primitive Methodist churches, Revs. J. W. Reed, J. H. Acornley and E. Humphries, pastors. Here she labored successively and successfully for two months, the Lord wonderfully blessed her and numbers were saved.

Mrs. Baker subsequently labored in the States of

Pennsylvania, Ohio, Virginia, Maryland, Delaware, New Jersey, New York and Connecticut, in connection with the Methodist Episcopal, Primitive Methodist, Methodist Protestant, United Brethren, Evangelical, Baptist, African Methodist Episcopal and African M. E. Zion churches, Nearly all evangelical denominations have shared in her labors. Preaching the gospel of Christ and lecturing on the story of her life.

In addition to those gentlemen already mentioned she has labored in the white churches with Revs. W. H. Yarrow, M. Harvey, H. G. Russell, J. Mason, J. A. McGreaham, G. Parker, J. A. James, T. James, D. Savage, T. Coburn, J. J. Arnaud and J. Finch, of the Primitive Methodist Church. Revs. Schaffer, Brown, Bleam, Bowman and Dr. Clemens of the Evangelical Association also Revs. H. C. McBride, W. H. Lawrence, T. P. Howard, Dr. McGregor and C. P. Corner of the M. E. Church, and Rev. J. White, of the Methodist Protestant Church, with a number more too numerous to mention.

In the colored churches she has labored with Revs. J. Davis, H. Davis, Arnold, Payton, Herbert, T. Hood, J. B. Morrison, Witmo, W. H. Bryant, Draper, J. S. Thompson, T. Moore, T. Gould, Bundy, W. Ralph, G. Miller, Bowser, J. Anderson, Norris, Stewart, Templeton, Brown, Taylor, W. Thompson, Heath and Jones.

Mrs. Baker's work has been indorsed by the following bishops of the A. M. E. Church: John M. Brown, Richard H. Cain, Jabez P. Campbell, M. D. Ward and H. M. Turner, from each of whom she has received authority to preach the Gospel.

She has held forth at quarterly meetings and camp-meetings, where in some cases she has had but a few humble listeners, and at other times she has addressed thousands. At Belfor, Ohio, at the camp-meeting, they took seven hundred and ninety dollars ($790.00) at the gate, at ten cents per head. It was said there were about fifteen thousand persons present, scarcely half of whom payed as they entered the grounds.

In the year 1889 she was appointed by the Philadelphia A. M. E. Conference to take charge of St. Paul's church on Tenth Street, in the city of Lebanon, Pa.

When she arrived she found the society at a very low ebb, overwhelmed with debt and such a few laborers that she had not only to bear all her own expences but by her own exertions pay off the debts which had been for so long accumulating on the church. This occupied all her time and was such a drain on her resources and energies, that she was of necessity compelled to neglect her own financial affairs at home. She removed to Lebanon, so that she might be enabled to give more attention to the church. During this enforced absence, the person who held the mortgage on her property foreclosed, and before she was aware of the transaction, the property was advertized and sold. Thus again her little all for which she had struggled so bravely and long, was gone.

The reader will remember that by industry a•d perseverance they had paid for their little home when the cruel slave hunters took off her husband into captivity again, and that she with indomitable courage mortgaged her house to redeem him, and for six years struggled to again free it from incumberance; when by an incendiary fire which took place during a raid by a party of rebels, it was burnt to the ground. Still she was not dispondent, but with commendable zeal, she rebuilt, and set about the task of paying a third time for it. Now however, while her trust in God is none the less than it has been in years past, and while she still believes that in His own wise provsdence He will open the way for her again, yet she feels that she has not the physical vigor she once had, her strength is failing. She purposes, however, to still struggle on, and if possible recover her home. She is open for engagements to preach special sermons, conduct revival missions, or lecture on the "story of her life." By this means, as well as by the sale of this book, she will continue to advance the interests of the church of Christ, and hasten the coming of Messiah's kingdom, while the financial benefit accruing to herself will help her in accomplishing her life long struggle of securing a home free of incumbrance, in which she can spend her declining days without being subject to the cankering care of difficulty and debt.

The results of her eighteen (18) years arduous labors, as far as can be tabulated, are that about five thousand (5000) persons have professed to realize salvation, and countless thousands of believers have been strengthened, and encouraged, and blessed.

CHAPTER VI.

PROSPECTS AND ANTICIPATIONS.

During her eighteen years work for Jesus, Mrs. Baker has not found everything pleasant at all times. She has had her trials and tribulations, which have been neither few nor small; some of these have been of a nature which could not have been avoided, but which are the common lot of all, both saint and sinner.

At one time while at Rupert, Pa., she was taken sick with a fever which had been raging like an epidemic in that section of country. The disease was fearfully fatal, the people being affected so that they became almost crazy and died off in great numbers. She started to her next appointment, Hazleton, Pa., feeling very sick in body—almost burning up with fever—but calling earnestly upon God for help and healing. And wonderful to relate by the time she arrived in Hazleton the fever had left her, and she was quite well. Thankfulness and praise welled up from her heart, her labors were honored of God, and much good was accomplished.

At another time while attending camp meeting at Smithfield, Ohio, she was stopping at a farm-house with a German family. The lady had been sick for nine months, the doctor had given her a small vial of medicine, for outward application, which though rank poison had so far benefited her that she was quite well. She gave Mrs. Baker this vial believing it would be of benefit for her throat; Mrs. Baker, however, determined not to touch it. On the Sabbath having preached twice, and being pressed to preach again in the evening, she thought she would take some drops the doctor had given her, for her throat, and taking the wrong bottle, swallowed a tea-spoon-full of the poison instead. She went to her appointment, though feeling very sick. returned home, and lay upon the bed all night in terrible pain, being unable to divest herself of her clothes. In the morning when she discovered she had taken the wrong bottle,—up to this time she knew not that she had made the mistake—she cried upon the Lord, pleaded the promises, took God at His word, and confidently believed that no harm would befall her. God honored her faith, destroyed the effect of the poison and fully restored her to her usual health. And O! how thankful she was to her beneficent Father for his goodness and grace.

Sickness has visited her family, her husband has been sick for the past nine years with chronic rheumatism, so much so that he is almost a helpless cripple. For about four years he was almost blind, and could only occasionally get little glimpses of light. During those four years he was treated at Wills Hospital,

Philadelphia, which occasioned his frequently visiting that institution. His sufferings have been protracted and intense. Until two years ago she had three children at home, when one of them enlisted in the United States army, and the other set sail on the sea of matrimony. One girl remains at home, attending school and ministering to the wants of her aged and suffering father.

Thus far the cash remuneration she has received for her services has been expended in the support of her family. and the payment of taxes, and interest on the nineteen hundred dollar ($1900.00) mortgage. which, until recently, hung like a pall over the little home she has struggled so heroically to save. The spiritual remuneration, however, cannot be expressed. She has realized Divine consolation, and blessed inspiration, and continues her labors in glorious anticipation of one day hearing the Master say "Come up higher."

Her sphere of usefulness is continually widening and opening out before her, larger churches, and richer congregations are seeking her services. Her time is almost wholly occupied in her beloved work. The summer season in camp-meetings, and the winter season in revival work, and all the time in leading sinners to Jesus, and believers into a higher, and richer, and more blessed experience.

The time she has to spend with her family is very

limited, and at longer or shorter intervals. She is, however, encouraged from a contemplation of the past to trust her beneficient Lord for the future.

As she goes from place to place endeavoring to bring out of God's treasury things new and old, and dropping the seeds of eternal truth, she prays for the blessing of the Divine husbandman on her labors, and anxiously looks for the first germs of that fruit, which when ripe, shall be gathered into the garner of God. And amid all her labors she constantly reflects on the way in which her heavenly parent has so lovingly guided and guarded her during her weary pilgrimage, and looks longingly

"Beyond the river
Where the surges cease to roll."

And she derives comfort from the thought, that when her probationary existence shall close, she will hear the glorious commendation "Well done," and going to the blessed mansion of light which her Saviour has so long had in reversion for her, she will bask in the glorious sunlight of his presence, and casting her given crown at his feet, will join the swelling chorus of the glorified throng in crowning him Lord of all.

"O that with yonder sacred throng
We at his feet may fall,
Join in the everlasting song,
And crown him Lord of all."

CHAPTER VII.

SERMONS.

"Behold the Man." John 19: 5.

I repeat the text, "Behold the Man," and in order to give you an idea of what gave rise to it, it is necessary to read the foregoing chapter [reads]

I now call attention to this man, mentioned in the text, and I wish you all to give special attention, as the constant labor of five months has almost broken me down. But a cry for help came from Macedonia, and here I am in response to that cry. I ask you all to pray. Do pray now as there is hard work to be done. Pray now if ever. Look to Jesus, and not to me; see him by faith as he hangs on the cross in the last act of atonement, and get the blessing of Jesus, the man of my text. I think of myself as resembling a horn; as nothing but a horn. You all know what a horn is and the uses that are made of it. The horn talks the sentiments of the person blowing it; it may sound the alarm of fire, of murder, or of danger; or it may give the glad sound of invitation to dinner to some half-starved soul who is hungering for the richness of the Master's table, where all may freely partake of the bread of everlasting life.

I will consider my text from three principal points:

1st. JESUS IN HIS POWER AND MIGHT.

2nd. JESUS IN HIS MEEKNESS.

3rd. JESUS IN HIS HUMILIATION.

Jesus was the Immaculate Son of God. Look at him as he was before the world was. When the wonders of creation were taking place, Jesus was there. When the Lord divided the waters from the dry land, and gave to the ocean its "metes and bounds," Jesus was there. When the darkness was driven away, and the glorious light beamed forth upon a new born world, Jesus was there. When the stars and planets were given their position, and orbits, in the immensity of space, Jesus was there. When God said "Let us make man in, our image, after our likeness," Jesus was there. When God created the fishes which swim in the mighty ocean, and the beautiful lakes, and the winding rivers, and the mountain streams, Jesus was there. When the beasts of the field were made, and the birds of the air sent forth their first notes of praise, Jesus was there. And dear friends I want you to hear to-day of his atonement for the sins of the world, and his ascension to heaven, where he has prepared a home for all his people. Glory to God for the atonement and for the resurrection.

On the sixth day of creation man was made in the image of God, male and female, and given the injunction to be fruitful, multiply, and replenish the earth.

Upon the empty air this earth was well balanced, and with joy Jesus saw the mansion where the sons of men should dwell. Yes, this same Jesus was with the Father at the foundation of the world, and shall be with him until the last, for he is the first and the last. Truly when the morning stars sang together and the sons of God shouted for joy, this great Saviour of mine was there, and he was yet there when God made man, and when man fell from that happy state of purity, and was driven from that beautiful garden, he was yet there with man in his unhappy condition, and promised him salvation. And when the angels made the search in heaven to find one that could open the book, and read the contents thereof, this same Jesus came forth as a lamb from under the altar. And when the question was asked "who is worthy to open the book?" Jesus was there, and as the angels listened, and John wept at the revelation, a voice was heard saying "weep not!" and the four and twenty elders sang a new song, saying, "Thou art worthy to take the book, and to open the seal thereof: for thou wast slain, and hast redeemed us to God by the blood, out of every kindred, and tongue, and people, and nation." And thank God, Jesus came, and redeemed us, and he has been with his church ever since, and he fights for her to-day.

Oh! how I do thank the Lord for the gift of his Son, and for the gift of the Holy Ghost, how he taught me to pray, and to read and understand his holy word. And as the poet says,

"Grace led my roving feet,
To tread the heavenly road,
And new supplies each hour I meet
While pressing on to God."

Grace found me when I was in my sins, and I was led to realize, and

"Know that the Lord is God alone;
He can create, and He destroy."

He is the foundation of all wisdom, upon the plain of wisdom this world was founded, and by the wisdom of God the sun, and moon, and stars, were made, and keep their regular course, and do not run one against the other. It is by the wisdom of God that the sun revolves in his place. It is by the wisdom of God we move and live. Oh! how I do thank him for his grace, and for his wisdom, that he has given unto me. I can say in truth, all glory belongs to him. Wisdom cried aloud. It is the voice of God's eternal Son. And deserves it no regard? I hear the voice of Jesus saying,

"I was my Father's chief delight,
His everlasting Son,
Before the first of all his works,
Or creation was begun;
Before the flying clouds,
Before the solid land,

Before the fields, before the flood;
I dwelt at his right hand."

When he adorned the skies, and built them; when he ordained the time for the sun to rise and set, and when he marshalled every star, I was there.

"When He poured out the sea,
And spread the roaring deep,
He gave the flood a firm decree,
And its own bounds to keep,"

But I want to speak of Jesus in his meekness.

Driven from Bethlehem by the wrath of a king, expelled from Nazareth by the violence of the people, received at Capernaum at first, only to be rejected at last, denied the protection of the three homes which was his by birth, by residence, and by adoption.

Jesus comes to Jerusalem to be betrayed, and to Calvary to die. Thirty years of retirement, and three years of public ministry, and yet all that the world will endure of its Messiah is not enough to secure him acceptance. It is not enough that he heals the sick, and feeds the hungry, and raises the dead. It is not enough that he speaks as never a man spake, and does the works which never a man did. It is not enough that he endures the contradiction of sinners with the meekness and majesty of infinite love. He must go down to a still lower depth of humiliation. He must take upon his soul the burden of a great agony, he must give his very life in sacrifice, before the strong walls of prejudice, and hatred, and unbelief will yield, and give him access to the hearts of men. We have something to learn from every step which he takes, as he approaches the great sacrifice of calvary. He had returned to Bethany for the nlght, the first decisive step towards the great sacrifice had been taken; he had showed himself the object of supreme interest to the multitude; and so had excited the envy and hatred of the customary leaders to the highest degree; he had come once more within their reach, they had already entered upon new plans to destroy him, it will take them yet four days to complete their dark counsel, and then when they demand the victim he will hold himself ready for the sacrifice.

Monday he comes back to the city, and made a still more striking exhibition of the power of his presence over men, by causing all that bought and sold in the temple to leave the holy place and take their tables and merchandise with them. At his command, hardened, selfish and calculating as they were, they could not withstand the authority with which he spake. The blind, the sick, and the lame, were brought to him in great numbers, and he healed them. The populace had been induced by threats or persuations to hold their peace, but the children in the temple took up the songs and cries of the previous day, and sang hossannah to the son of David; When the priests and the scribes demanded his authority for what he did, he put them to shame before all the people by the wisdom of his reply. And when evening was come he went back to Bethany leaving them still more enraged, and intent upon seeking his life.

Tuesday he comes again to the city; This was the third and last successive day of his public teaching. His enemies assailed him in greater numbers, and with greater subtility than ever before, when one was silenced, another would renew the assault, all alike endeavour to ensnare him in his words, and to draw from him some expression which could be used as an accusation against him. before the magistrate; But all in vain, they only induce him io set before the people by new parables, and in a more awful light, the dreadful doom which they would bring on themselves on the temple, and the holy city, by thus rejecting the Messiah, He pronounced in their hearing the most fearful woes upon the blind and bigoted leaders of the people, and then left them.

This is enough, the priests and scribes will see to it that the dreaded voice of their reprover shall not be heard in the courts of the temple, or in the streets any more. To night the great councel will meet in secret session, at the palace of their high priest, and the betrayer will be there to bargain for the reward of his iniquity in delivering Jesus into their hands.

On his way out to Bethany Jesus paused before passing the ridge of Olives, and sat down with his disciples over against the temple, to look back upon Jerusalem for the last time. The sun was setting, and the whole city, with the surrounding vallies, and the hill-sides which were covered with the camps of pilgrims, lay beneath him. In the evening light, the history of a thousand years, the divine oracles speaking by a thousand voices, the monuments of prophets, patriarchs, and Kings, the visitation of Angels, the miracolous interposition in judgement, and in blessing, by the offering of Isaec, and the building of the temple, was presented to him, as he looked upon Moriah and Zion; and as he heard the murmur, and the evening song of a million people gathered within, and around the walls of the whole city.

Now my hearers, was it possible here on earth to find another scene of such commanding interest. as that which lay beforn the eyes of Jesus, when he turned to look upon Jerusalem for the last time. There he sat until the sun went down, and the stars shone, and the already risen moon grows bright over the mountain. There he poured forth in the most solemn and touching words, prophecy, and warning, and instrction, concerning the desolation of Jerusalem, the depression oi the jewish people, the preaching of the gospel to all nations, and his own final coming to judge the world in righteousness. And he closes this the most awful, and sublime of all his discourses with distinct and solemn declaration that after two days he should be betrayed, and crucified. Then he resumes his walk to Bethany, and rested for the night.

The whole of the following day, Wednesday, he spent in retirement, at his chosen and quiet home in Bethany, his public work was done, and while his enemies where completing their plans, for his destruction, he would take a little time to gird up his soul for the trial of mockery and scourging, and for the crowning agony of the cross. He would need the repose of two quiet days to prepare himself for the last sleepless night, and for the long tortures of the last dreadful day. When he leaves the quiet village for the last time on Thursday, he goes to be betrayed and crucified. His whole body, and soul, and spirit will be tasked with the most exhausting intensity, until he bows his head in death at the ninth hour on Friday afternoon. As the evening of Thursday draws near, Jesus sets forth upon his last walk with his disciples, before his passover. We do not know what words of farewell were spoken when he parted with his beloved friends at Bethany, they fondly hoping to see him return to lodge with them as before, and he well knowing that his next resting place would be the grave. We are not told what he said to his disciples as he walked with them up the same steep, or down the same descent of Olives, where the multitudes hailed his coming with hozannas, four days before. We do not know whether in silence, or with weeping, or with comfortable words. He passed Gethsemanie, and across the brook Kidron, and climbing up the ascent to what is now called St. Stephen's gate. And from the moment of his arrival at the upper chamber in the city, where the passover was prepared, we may well imagine that his countenance wore an unwonted tenderness and solemnity, and that the wondering disciples saw the foreshadowing signs of the final agony upon him. The awful history of this last night, and the following day, will be studied with wonder and adoration, by angels and redeemed men forever. We can now only recite its most familiar facts, as a preparation for the lesson of the cross.

I want now to speak of Jesus in his humiliation.

He was just about to complete his earthly humiliation, and to return to the throne of heaven, with all power in his name, and all glory upon his head. Jesus teaches his disciples the greatest lesson of humiliation.

While they were contending with each other for the promise of the highest place in his kingdom, he girded himself as a servant, and washed the feet of them that called him Lord.

He was just about to offer himself, the pure and spotless Lamb of God, in the great and only sacrifice for sin; He finished the sacrifice of four thousand years, as he eat the passover with his diciples. This was one of the national festivals which the Jewish people observed from the days of Moses.

Jesus started a new dispensation and instituted a memorial service, to be kept by his followers of every nation, to the end of time. As he looks around upon the chosen company of his disciples, the dark shadow of coming treachery over shadows and troubles his soul, and groaning within himself, he nerves his heart, to make the sad declaration, "Verily, verily, I say unto you that one of you shall betray me." The disclosure makes the company of the disciples, and the presence of the Master, intolerable to the traitor, and he goes immediately out.

It is night in the streets of blinded and abandoned Jerusalem, night in the councels of the enemies of Jesus, night in the soul of the betrayer, night upon the path which he must tread, for no sooner had the dark shadow of the traitor left the room, than the troubled cloud passed from the face of Jesus. and he turns to his remaining disciples with the light of heaven in his look, and he pours forth his soul in words of love, of counsel, and of prayer, which shall outlive the languish of earth, and shall be sung by happy voices to the music of heaven. He himself joins with his disciples in singing the great Hallelujah song, with which Israel had closed the passover for a thousand years. Praise the Lord, all ye nations; praise him all ye people; for his merciful kindness is great towards us, his mercy endures forever.

He knows where the betrayer will expect to meet him, at the midnight hour, and there he goes that he may be ready, when the officers and soldiers come with Judas for their guide, to take him once more through their silent streets, and out of their eastern gate, and across the Kidron valley, beneath the shadows of the olive trees which are cast in the full light of the moon. Jesus goes to his place of prayer, the betrayer knows the spot, for Jesus had often been there before with his disciples.

To this day in spite of all intervening changes, the scene can be identified with reasonable accuracy. And it is the most solemn and affecting of all the holy places in Palestine. The aged olive trees, with gnarled and distorted trunks, appearing as if bent and twisted by the tortureies of centuries, are undoubtedly the most fitting monuments, if any be needed to make the ground sacred.

Whilst waiting for the armed band to appear, Jesus is again troubled in spirit, and his soul is bowed down under the weight of a more awful and mysterious agony than had ever come upon him before. He is overcome with a strange amazement, an inexplicable and shuddering dread, a horror of great darkness, and an exceeding great sorrow, embittered with more than the bitterness of death; the sweat wrung out by the inward torture, falls in blood drops to the ground. Thrice he prays in the same words, that the cup may pass from him.

When the armed band appears, and he goes forth to give himself up, his troubled countenance at once assumes so much of its serene and godlike majesty that the hardened soldiers, are struck to the ground with awe, but the delay is only momentary, he offers himself again, and they bind him, and lead him away. It is now past midnight, and from this time forward the course of the events in this awful history, ran swiftly on to the closing scene on the cross.

Walking painfully with bound hands, amidst the rude and merciless mob, Jesus was hurried up the steep pass, through the city gates to the house of Annas, not for a formal trial did they bring him there, but only that the old father-in-law of the high priest the man whose counsel was of the highest authority in the nation, might have the dreadful satisfaction of seeing Jesus of Nazereth a prisoner.

Then out again, into the dark, narrow streets, finding their way, only, by the uncertain light of lanterns and torches, they hurry their unresisting victim, with insult and mockery to the palace of Caiaphas. There he is questioned by the high priest, testified against by false witnesses, smitten by the officers, reviled by the whole assembly, condemned to death by the counsel, and still after the decision kept exposed to every form of contemptious speech, and personal abuse, till the breaking of the day. The morning of Friday breaks, a day to be recognized as the greatest of all the days of time, a day to be remembered as long as redeemed souls can remember the sacrifice which purchased for them a blessed immortality. The sentence of the sanhedrim must now be confirmed and executed by the civil power, or it will be of no effect, and the enemies of Jesus hurry on their dreadful work, with such malignant and impetuous zeal, that the prisoner, who was seized in Gethsemanie, without the city, at midnight, has been led to and fro, through many streets, to four different places or tribunals, has been arranged before the high priest, twice before the sanhedrim, twice before Pilate, once before Herod, once robed and crowned in mockery, twice scourged, everywhere mocked and condemned, led outside of the city wall, and by nine o'clock, when the sun is looking over the ridge of olivet, in the deep valley of Kidron, he is already nailed to the cross. In six hours more, the most momentous hours in the world's history, the awful tragedy is finished, and the Incarnate Son of God bows his head in death. It is all one act, one mysterious and infinate passion, from the agony in Gethsemanie, to the last bitter cry upon calvary.

The betrayal, the arrest, the arraignment, the false

accusation, the mockery, the denial, the scourging, the final sentence, and its execution, must all unite to make up the meaning of that most sacred and awful mystery, the cross of Christ. The most sorrowful procession that ever moved on this earth, was that in which Jesus was led out of the city, to be crucified, amidst the wails of the daughters of Jerusalem, and the mockery of the multitude who clamored for his death.

SERMON II.

JESUS WEEPING OVER JERUSALEM.

"And when he was come near, he beheld the city, and wept over it." Luke 19: 41.

In the gardens and vineyards on all the hill-sides facing the city, are encamped thousands and thousands who had come up to the great national feast, all this vast population are moved at his coming; and the multitude around him lifted up their voices in cries of welcome so loud, that some within the city walls, hearing the sound, said, the world has gone after him. At this moment, of supreme triumph, Jesus weeps; not for himself, although he well knows, that before that week should close, the hozannas of the multitude would give place to the cry, "crucify him, crucify him." Not because his work had failed, and his mission must close in defeat, and disappointment, He weeps over doomed and blind Jerusalem, because she knows not the time of her visitation; He weeps, because, the last and utmost appeal which he can make, to the hearts of men, by his death on the cross, will still be rejected by many, to their own distruction; He weeps, because, many by continuance in impenitence and unbelief will bring on themselves wrath unto the uttermost, when they might have been saved with a full and everlasting salvation. And so Jesus began the great work of his passion, with triumph, and with tears, the earthly triumph will soon be passed, but it will give place to another, when he shall have led captivity captive, and the angelic host shall form the dazzling procession, and the everlasting gates of heaven, shall be lifted up, that the King of glory may come in. The sorrow with which Jesus wept over Jerusalem, shall give place to joy when he shall look back upon the travail of his soul, and be satisfied, with the fruits of his toil and suffering. From this time forward Jesus persued the open and avowed course, which he knew must bring him to the cross. For a time he had avoided publicity, and had kept himself out of the reach, of those who were plotting together, at Jerusalem, to put him to death. But now the work of teaching is done, the evidences of his Divine Mission are complete, and he goes voluntarily, to put himself in the way of his enemies, that their malice may become the instrument, of completing the great sacrifice for the world's redemption. Descending the western slope of Olivet, and crossing the Kidron, Jesus entered the city by the gate of St. Stephens, and went up and showed himself in the courts of the temple, with the singing and shouting multitude still around him. The whole city was moved, the scribes read the law with none to listen, and the priests were left alone with the evening sacrifice, for everybody had joined the eager crowd, that was swaying and surging to and fro, in their endeavor, to see, and to hear the prophet of Nazareth. Having looked around silently upon all things, Jesus left the temple, and the city. His first entrance into Jerusalem on the solemn week of his passion, has the appearance of a triumph. He had walked up the wild and dreary road from Jerico, and from the fords of the Jordan to Bethany, and had spent his last earthly sabbath at the house of his friends, in that mountain village. It was the week of the passover, and multitudes of pilgrims where on their way from Galilee, to keep the great festival in the holy city. Some remained with him at Bethany. On the day of rest many passed over the brow of Olivet, and encamped in the gardens, and orchards, on the western slope of the mountain, everywhere spreading the tidings that the prophet of Nazareth was but two miles off at Bethany, and would appear in the city, before the feast had closed. On the afternoon of sunday, the first day of the Jewish week, Jesus renewed his Journey, accompanied by a great multitude from Bethany, who were eager to witness his reception into the city. He set forth knowingly and willingly to meet his death. When the new life of the year had come, and the whole land was green and blossoming, with the glory of spring, taking the most traveled road, over the southern ridge of Olivet, he was joined by a still greater multitude, who had heard of his coming, and had gone forth from the camp on the hill-side, and from the streets of Jerusalem, to meet him. When the two great processions met, the one which from the direction of the city turned and went before, and the other which started out from Bethany followed, with Jesus in the midst, and both united in rending the air with shouts of joy, which were heard in all the streets, and on all the hill-sides around and about Jerusalem. Branches were broken from the palms, by the way-side, and hastilly braded into mattings to carpet the road, others still more enthusiastic, threw off their outer garments, and spread them in tee way to be trodden upon by the beast that bore the Son of David. And so far were the excited multitudes from exaggerating the greatness of the occasion, by their shouts, and demonstrations of joy, that Jesus himself said, that the stones would immediately cry out, were the people to hold their peace. Rounding the southern ridge of the mountain, and coming out upon a level platform of the rock, Jesus beheld across the deep revine of the Kidson, the whole magnificent city in one full and instantaneous view. Conspicious above everything else, the golden domes, and Pinnicals, of the temple, rise before him, like the flame of a mighty sacrifice. The whole mass of compact streets, and stone houses, within the walls, are crowded with people, and while they shout hosannas, Jesus returns to Bethany for the night. And now the first decisive step towards the great sacrifice had been taken.

Christ died for our sins according to the Scriptures. Christ's death was not the beginning of his sufferings, it was the end of them. Without his death his work would not have been finished. It was the great crowning event of which much is said in the word of God. We ought to think much of it. Let us briefly look at a few things respecting it.

1st. CHRIST'S DEATH WAS REAL.

Some have contended that it was only apparent and shadowy, and that Jesus Christ did not actually die. His enemies said he was dead, the soldiers around his cross were so sure that he was dead that they brake not his legs, his friends and disciples so firmly believed that he was dead, that they were cast into the deepest gloom. Christ really died.

2nd. CHRIST'S DEATH WAS ANTICIPATED BY HIMSELF; IN FACT HE HIMSELF FORETOLD IT.

He knew it by his own omniscience. He well understood the prophets and they said he must die. He died for our sins according to the Scripture. He so fully anticipated his own death and the manner of it, that it cast a pall of sadness over his whole life. He says "I have a baptism to be baptised with, and how am I straitened until it be accomplished." Luke xii: 50.

From men, the time and manner of their death is concealed, they may commonly hope that it will not be in such torment as that that our Lord endured. But he knew the time and manner in which he should die. He died his death as it were a thousand times.

3rd. CHRIST'S DEATH WAS VOLUNTARY.

This was a great point. Had Christ died unwillingly his blood would have availed nothing for us. On this point the Scriptures are very clear, in one of the Messianic prophecies, Christ speaking on the subject of the great sacrifice he was to offer, says; "I delight to do Thy will O God." Psalm xl: 8. And during his stay on earth he repeatedly said that if he chose he could avoid dying. When Pilate said, "knowest thou not that I have power to crucify thee?" Jesus answered: "Thou couldest have no power at all against me except it were given thee from above." John xix: 11. Even before that he had said, "I lay down my life, that I may take it again, no man taketh it from me but I lay it down of myself." John x: 17. 18. Still later he said "thinkest thou that I cannot now pray to my Father and he shall presently give me more than twelve legions of angels?" Matt. xxvi: 53. Nothing is more clear than that our Saviour died voluntarily, yet he died a violent death. In fact it was exceedingly violent. He was put to death in a manner expressive of the greatest hatred by his enemies. On the day of pentecost Peter proved that he had been murdered. "Him being delivered by the determinate counsel and foreknowledge of God ye have taken and by wicked hands have crucified and slain." Acts ii: 23. Christ had full power over his own life but he permitted his foes to crucify him.

4th. CHRIST'S DEATH WAS SHAMEFUL.

Hanging has always been a death of ignomy, and the death of the cross has always been the most shameful, no citizen nor even a liberated slave could be crucified in the Roman Empire. That kind of death was for servile criminals alone. This manner of putting criminals to death was continued until Constantine abolished it in honor of our Lord's death. Every mark of shame attended our Saviour's death. His raiment was taken from him, he was put to death between two thieves, one of whom confessed that they deserved death, no mark of respect was shown him, all was cold contempt, but he endured the cross despising the shame. The death of our Saviour was accursed, indeed he was made a curse for us, for it is written "cursed is every one that hangeth on the tree." Gal. iii: 13. It was only in this way that he could redeem us from the curse of the law, it rested on us till he bore it in our room and stead. We may never know the half or the thousandth part of what is meant by his being made a curse. In many respects his sufferings were the most mysterious ever witnessed, that awful wrath of God which was due to us fell on him.

5th. CHRIST'S DEATH WAS INCONCEIVABLY PAINFUL.

The theory of death by crucifixion was to torture

men to death by nervous distress, some blood indeed was shed, but not enough to take life. If ever there was such a thing as dying by inches it was when men hung upon the cross. There was no change of posture in that death it was slow and lingering there was never any death like it.

6th. CHRIST'S DEATH WAS SOLITARY.

His friend John, his mother, and some other women, were there looking at the awful spectacle but they were filled with grief and dismay, not one of them seems to have said a word to cheer or comfort him. He saw what Simeon had foretold, a sword piercing the soul of his mother, everything like solace was withheld.

Often through life he had enjoyed the light of his Father's face, but in his agony, even that was taken and he cried out, "My God, my God, why hast thou forsaken me." Neither man or woman, nor angel nor God stood by him, he trod the wine-press alone.

7th. CHRIST'S DEATH WAS WITHOUT COMFORT.

We have seen how he was forsaken, when he said "I thirst." They gave him vinegar, mingled with gall, a potion suited to increase his torment. After a while they offered him a stupifying dose, but he declined it. Usually the dying are left to die quickly but his murderers taunted him. and the soldiers who executed him went to gambling at the foot of the cross, all was coarse brutality in his foes. The pain of our

Saviour's body was but a small part of his suffering, his agony was chiefly in his soul. The sufferings of his soul were the soul of his sufferings. Before the kiss of betrayal, before his arrest or trial, he said, "my soul is exceeding sorrowful even unto death." Jehovah had said, "Awake O sword against my shepherd and against the man that is my fellow." Zech. xiii: 7. O that death! None but the Saviour who endured it, and God who inflicted it, knew what it was.

8th. Christ's Death was Expiatory.

He died for our sins, he had no sins of his own, he never displeased God, his soul was holy, but he took our place under the law which we had broken. The Bible is explicit on this point, "surely he hath borne our griefs and carried our sorrows...... he was wounded for our transgressions, he was bruised for our iniquities, the chastisement of our peace was upon him, and with his stripes we are healed." Isa. 53: 5,6. Blessed be God.

The wine-press has been trodden, the work of expiation is finished, justice is satisfied, the law is magnified, God is glorified, the Scriptures are true, the prophecies and histories of our Lord so fully agree, the types and the antitypes so perfectly correspond that if we had no proof of the Divine origin of the Bible but that furnished by the prophecies and life of our Lord, the argument would be clear and full. There are so many things of this sort and of so marked a kind that we know we have God's word when we read the Bible. How light are all our crosses, what are they all compared with the sufferings of Christ? If we believe in Jesus there is not a drop of wrath in any cup of bitterness ever put into our hands. Whatever may come upon us it is not fit to be spoken of on the same day on which we speak of our Saviour's death.

9th. CHRIST'S DEATH IS A GREAT ARGUMENT AGAINST SIN.

If it was of so malignant a nature as to bring on our surety and substitute such dreadful agonies surely we ought to crucify it. How shall we who are dead to sin live any longer therein. We need not accuse the Jews, Pilate or the Romans, it was our sins that caused the death of Christ. O let us hate our sins and put them all to death. Want of faith in Christ is a great sin, after all he has done and suffered for us to boubt his love and willingness to save, or to reject his grace is a wickedness that has few equals. If Christ has not proved his love and pity for men it cannot be proven that there is such a thing as love or pity. We cannot have, and we need no fairer argument for love to our brethren, than is drawn from Christ's love in dying for us. It is conclusive, "Hereby perceive we the love of God because he laid down his life for us, and we ought to lay down our lives for the brethren." 1 John 3: 16. See also John 13; 34; 15: 12, and Rom 16: 3, 4. The confidence and composure of believers in Christ is well founded. Conscience as well as Scripture says that "without the shedding of blood there is no remission." and conscience as well as Scripture, says, "the blood of Christ cleanseth from all sin." The destroying angel never entered a house in Egypt where the blood of the paschal lamb was sprinkled on the lintels of the door.--The scarlet thread in Rahabs house protected her from all harm at the fall of Jericho, so all the prisoners go forth by the blood of the covenant. In it, and in him who shed it, we may have the most abundant joy. All is safe when the blood of remission is applied. We need no more atonement than we find in the great sacrifice of calvary. "No wonder that he who believeth in Jesus and sees anything of the fullness of his grace and mercy seek no other Saviour, desires no other intercessor but Christ alone.